Puzzle Splash

CONTENTS

Crow and the Pitcher	page 4
Water Quiz: True or False?	page 18

NATIONAL GEOGRAPHIC School Publishing
Hampton-Brown

Words with Long i

Look at each picture. Read the words.

Example:

dime

bedtime

High Frequency Words
after
away
before
carry
does
give
put
through

Key Words

Look at the pictures. Read the sentences.

Water for Pets

1. My pet **does** not have water.
2. So I **carry** a jug to the tap.
3. **After** I **put** water in the jug, I walk **away**.
4. Outside, I walk **through** my gate and see a lot of pets.
5. I **give** water to all the pets.
6. **Before** long, there is no water left!

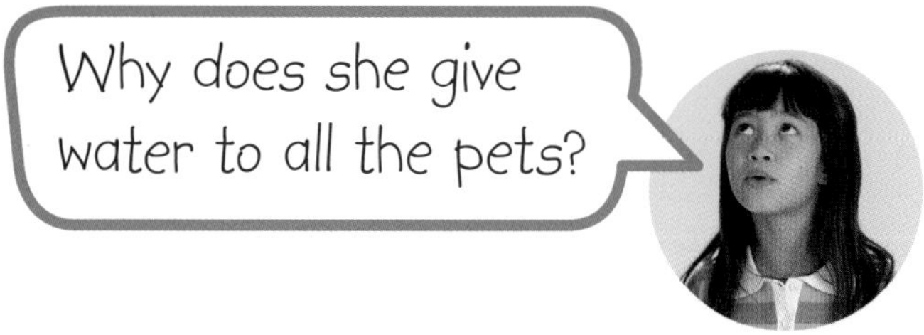

Phonics Games

NGReach.com

Crow and the Pitcher

by Rowan Obach
illustrated by Peter Grosshauser

Crow glides through the hills. He has not had water in a long time. He must have water!

Then Crow spots a pitcher and dives down to check. It has a bit of water inside.

The top of this pitcher is not wide. Crow can stick his bill in, but he can't get the water.

Crow strikes the pitcher to make it tip over. He swipes at it and tugs it. But he cannot get it to tip on its side. It is too big.

Crow stops to think. Can he bite the pitcher and crack it? He bites with his bill.

The pitcher is too strong. It will not crack.

Crow does not quit. He must get a drink. After a while, he spots some stones.

Crow can carry a stone in his bill. He brings a stone to the pitcher and drops it in.

Crow gets one more stone and drops it in. Then he gets one more. Time after time, Crow drops in stones.

Before long, the water in the pitcher rises. It rises up and up. Crow stops and admires his trick.

At last, he can put his bill in the pitcher and get a big drink. The water gives him a good feeling. He smiles.

Crow glides away in the sunshine. He has gotten a fine lesson in life:

Little by little does the trick. ❖

Words with Long ī

Read these words.

dive	sunshine	hide	glide
grass	invite	wish	pond

Find the words with long **i**.
Use letters to build them.

d i v e

Talk Together

Choose words from the box to tell your partner what the duck can do.

The duck can dive in the pond.

1.

2.

3.

o

o_e

Words with Long o

Look at each picture. Read the words.

Example:

g**o**

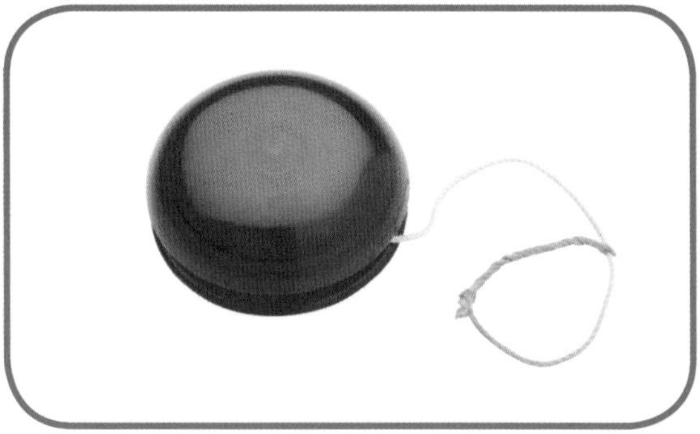

y**o**-y**o**

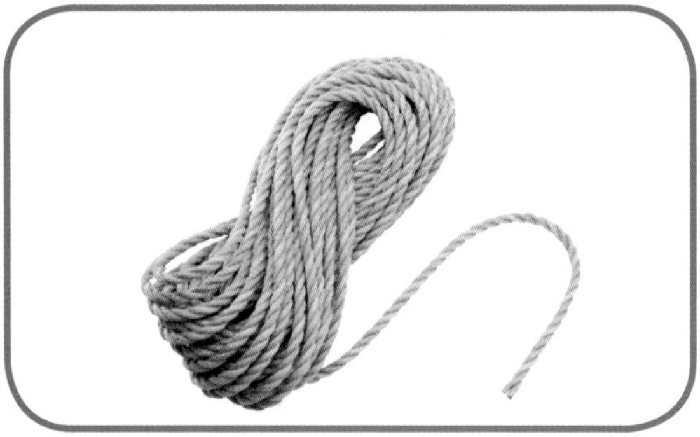

r**o**p**e**

h**o**m**e**

gl**o**b**e**

flagp**o**l**e**

High Frequency Words
after
away
before
carry
does
give
put
through

Key Words

Look at the pictures. Answer the questions.

Which One?

1. Which one can take long trips **through** hot sand?
2. Which one can **give** a tug and **put** its legs in water?
3. Which one can **carry** **away** things on its back?
4. **Before** a trip, which one will swim?
5. **After** a long trip, which one will drink water?
6. Which one **does** not have a hump?

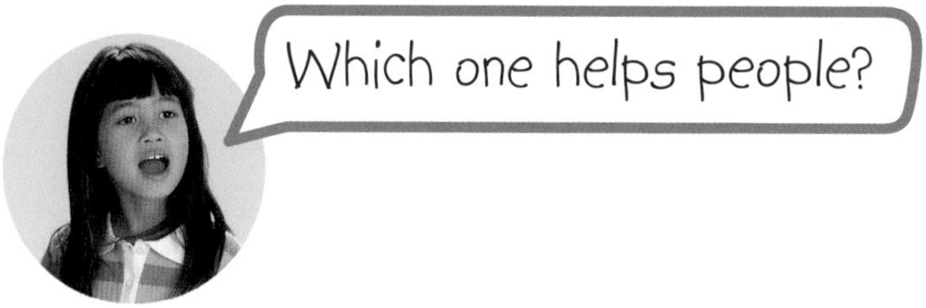

Phonics Games
NGReach.com

Water Quiz: True or False?

by Winston White

How well do you suppose you know water plants and animals? Very well?

Before you say *yes* or *no*, stop! I propose a quiz. After you take it, you can say *yes* or *no*.

True or false? A cactus saves water inside.

True A cactus lives in a spot with a bit of water close by. It puts its roots into the sand to get to this water.

A cactus saves water in its stem. This stem has a wax-like skin that will not let water out.

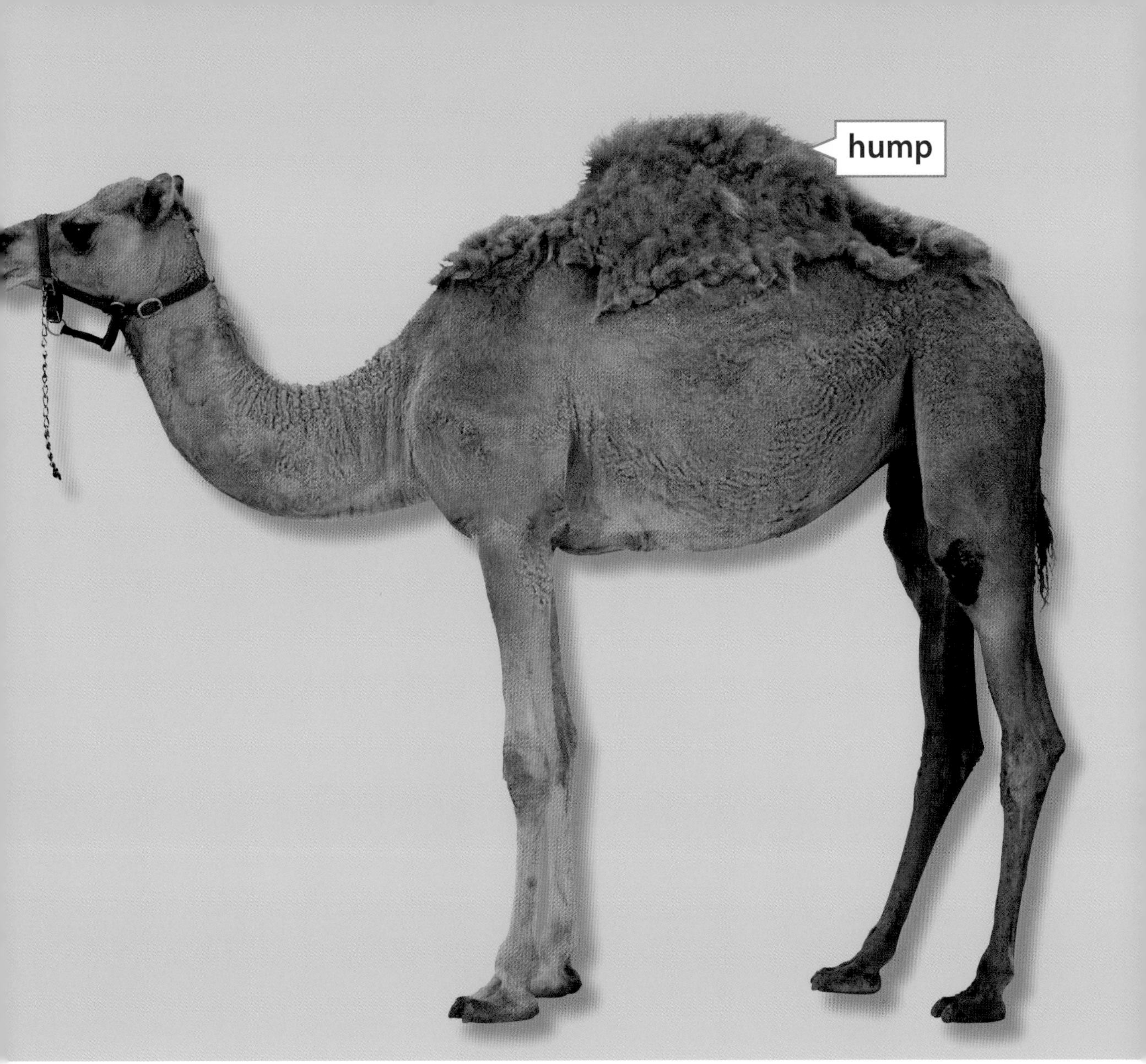

True or false? A camel saves water in its hump.

False A camel does not save water in its hump. But it can go for a long time without water. It can carry fat in its hump. It uses this fat when it cannot get a thing to eat.

True or false? Some insects can walk on water.

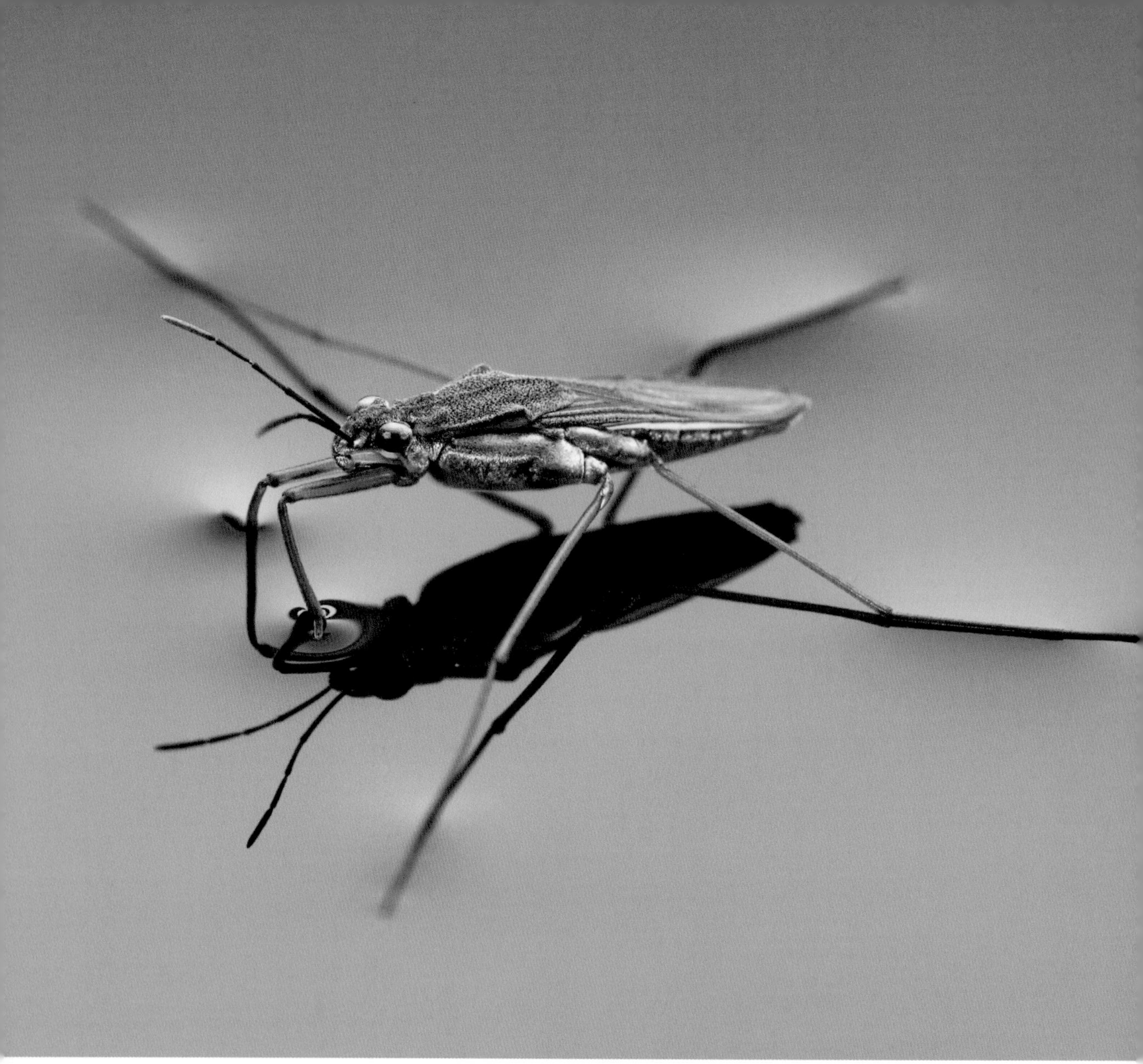

True This insect can walk on water. Hairs on those long legs trap air. The air gives the insect the skill to skip on top of its water home.

True or false? This fish can walk on land.

True This fish *can* walk on land! It uses fins on its strong chest to drag itself up a slope. On land, this fish gets air through its gills and skin.

True or false? Plants in a lake are stuck on the bottom of the lake.

False Some lake plants rest on top with roots that hang down. Some are pests that choke up a lake, which is bad for lake plants and animals.

So, how well did you do on this quiz? ❖

Words with Long o̲

Read these words.

plant	doze	poke	stone	trombone
yo-yo	shade	sun	go	suppose

Find the words with long **o**.
Use letters to build them.

p o k e

Talk Together

Choose words from the box to tell your partner about the camel.

It will go under the shade.

1. 

2. 

3. 

What Is It?

Look at the pictures with a partner. Take turns reading the clues. They will give you hints.

1. It does not live close to water. It lives away from water.

2. It has a wide stem that traps water inside.

3. This stem has a hole. The hole is a home!

4 Do not get too close! It has spines that can poke through skin or put holes in fabric.

5 You can admire its buds.

6 So, after reading those hints, what do you suppose it is?

Answer: It is a cactus!

Acknowledgments
Grateful acknowledgment is given to the authors, artists, photographers, museums, publishers, and agents for permission to reprint copyrighted material. Every effort has been made to secure the appropriate permission. If any omissions have been made or if corrections are required, please contact the Publisher.

Photographic Credits
CVR (b) Polka Dot Images/Jupiterimages. (t) FLPA/Jeremy Early/age fotostock. **2** (br) Cheryl Casey/Shutterstock. (l) GreenStockCreative/Alamy Images. **3** Liz Garza Williams/Hampton-Brown/National Geographic School Publishing. **15** (bc) Insuratelu Gabriela Gianina/Shutterstock. (bl) siloto/Shutterstock. (br) Tony Alt/Shutterstock. (t) Liz Garza Williams/Hampton-Brown/National Geographic School Publishing. **16** (bl) Thinkstock Images/Jupiterimages. (brc) Linda Johnsonbaugh/Shutterstock. (br, cl, trc) PhotoDisc/Getty Images. (tl) R McKown/Shutterstock. **17** (b) Liz Garza Williams/Hampton-Brown/National Geographic School Publishing. (r) Carsten Peter/National Geographic Image Collection. (tl) Michael Sheehan/Shutterstock. **18** Michael Nichols/National Geographic Image Collection. **19** Witold Ryka/iStockphoto. **20** Image Source Pink/Alamy Images. **21** PhotoDisc/Getty Images. **22** Sean Randall/iStockphoto. **23** Bianca Lavies/National Geographic Image Collection. **25** Maximilian Weinzierl/Alamy Images. **26** age fotostock/SuperStock. **27** Nikita Tiunov/Shutterstock. **28** Deborah Benbrook Photography/Alamy Images. **29** (bc) Eitan Simanor/Alamy Images. (bl) imagebroker/Alamy Images. (br) Robert Churchill/iStockphoto. (t) Liz Garza Williams/Hampton-Brown/National Geographic School Publishing. **30** (b) Lewis W. Walker/National Geographic Image Collection. (c) Robert Glusic/PhotoDisc/Getty Images. (t) Bates Littlehales/National Geographic Image Collection. **31** (c) Darla Hallmark/Shutterstock. (t) Dgrilla/Shutterstock.

Illustrator Credits
2-3, **20** Constanza Basaluzzo; **4-14** Peter Grosshauser

National Geographic School Publishing
Hampton-Brown
www.NGSP.com

Printed in the USA.
Quad Graphics, Leominster, MA

ISBN: 978-0-7362-8065-5

16 17 18 19
10 9 8